A Log's Life

By WENDY PFEFFER

Illustrated by

ROBIN BRICKMAN

Simon & Schuster Books for Young Readers

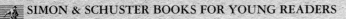

SIMON & SCHUSTER BOOKS FOR YOUNG READERS
An imprint of Simon & Schuster Children's Publishing Division
1230 Avenue of the Americas, New York, New York 10020. Text copyright © 1997 by Wendy Pfeffer.
Illustrations copyright © 1997 by Robin Brickman. All rights reserved including the right of reproduction
in whole or in part in any form. SIMON & SCHUSTER BOOKS FOR YOUNG READERS is a trademark of
Simon & Schuster. Book design by Paul Zakris. The text for this book is set in 17-point
Garamond Three Bold. Manufactured in China. 20 19 18 17 16 15 14 13
LIBRARY OF CONGRESS CATALOGING-IN-PUBLICATION DATA
Pfeffer, Wendy, S.   A log's life / by Wendy Pfeffer ; illustrations by Robin Brickman.
 p.   cm.   Summary: Introduction to the life cycle of a tree.
ISBN 0-689-80636-1   1. Forest ecology—Juvenile literature. 2. Oak—Juvenile literature.
3. Animals—Food—Juvenile literature. {1. Oak. 2. Trees. 3. Forest ecology. 4. Ecology.}
I. Brickman, Robin, ill. II. Title.   QH541.5.F6P45 1997   574.5'2642—dc20 95-30020

Acknowledgments

*Robin Brickman would
like to thank the following
people for their help:*

Nathan Erwin
MANAGER OF THE INSECT ZOO
SMITHSONIAN INSTITUTION

Thom Smith
THE BERKSHIRE MUSEUM

THESE MEMBERS OF THE UNIVERSITY OF
MASSACHUSETTS DEPARTMENT OF ENTOMOLOGY:

T. Michael Peters
John Stoffolano
Mike Desena
Faith Thayer

This book is dedicated to all children who look for little creatures under rocks and rotting logs, but especially to Andrew, Tim, Jaime, Eddie John, Laura Ann, Gary, Marisa, Jonathan, Christopher, and Kailyn

—W. P.

For Jefferson, who knows our roots, and loves to walk in the forest

—R. B.

A note from the illustrator:

I made the illustrations by cutting, painting, sculpting, and then gluing pieces of watercolor paper together. There are no found objects or real or preserved specimens in the artwork. With the exception of an occasional use of human hair, the illustrations consist only of painted paper and glue.

Deep in a forest a great
oak tree stands.

A family of squirrels lives
in a hole in its trunk.
A porcupine chews on its branches.
A colony of carpenter ants nests
under the outer bark.

A woodpecker pecks
at the rough bark,
searching for insects.
He spears one,
devours it,
and hunts for more.

Wood-boring beetles burrow under the bark,
   chewing wood and
      leaving tunnels.
Water and air seep into the tunnels.

Toadstools and other fungi
   such as mildew, molds,
     and mushrooms
       sprout in these damp places.

Slugs and snails crawl
   up the tree trunk
     into the tunnels
       and eat the fungi.

One stormy day a strong wind whips through the forest.
The old oak bends with every gust.

Rain pelts its branches.
Wind tosses its leaves through the air.
Lightning flashes and sizzles down its trunk.

A thunderous crack startles the porcupine sleeping nearby.
The tall oak begins to topple.
Squirrels feel the trembling,
and scramble out of their hole.

One strong gust of blustery wind
tears the great oak's roots from the ground.
The tree crashes down, shaking the forest floor.
Branches break. Limbs splinter. Leaves scatter.

Now it's a giant log.

Soon the storm stops
and the sun comes out.
An umbrella of leaves
and tangled branches block the sunshine
from the forest floor.
The porcupine comes out of its den.
Squirrels scamper to see the old hole
that was once their home.

Under the log ants rush about,
carrying white bundles of babies.
A spider crawls through cracks and crevices,
searching for a dry spot to place her egg sac.
Millipedes settle between the log and the wet ground.
For now, they are safe from the spider.
Termites soon discover the fallen log
and move in.
They not only eat the rotting wood,
they lay their eggs there, too.

For three or four years, through
hot, cold, wet, and dry seasons,
ants, beetles, fungi, slugs,
snails, spiders, millipedes,
and termites
live in the log.

One winter the porcupine's
hollow log collapses.
He moves into
the oak log, too.

In the spring click beetles snap and click their bodies
and flip high in the air before settling in the log.
Salamanders, frightened by the noise and
sudden movements, dart under the log
for safety . . . and stay.

In the summer pill bugs and slugs crawl inside
the cool, moist log to keep from drying out.
Pill bugs eat dead leaves. Salamanders eat the pill bugs.
Slugs slip out at night and eat almost anything.

The old log provides both food
and shelter for the millipedes.
They eat decaying plants and trees.
But spiders eat the millipedes.

Several more years of hot, cold, wet, and dry seasons pass.

Time, weather, and the chewing, pecking, boring, and tunneling of many animals and insects make the inside of the log spongy.

The outer bark becomes soft and damp, and gradually it falls to the ground.

Wood-boring insects have no wood to bore.
They find another log.
    The woodpecker hunts for other trees to peck.
    Spiders spin their webs in drier spots.
    And the porcupine moves
to a more solid log.

Slowly, a lush green blanket
of moss carpets the rotting log.
Its thick roots break down the wood.
Over the next few years the log crumbles.

What is left looks like dirt.
It feels like dirt. It smells like dirt.
It *is* dirt.

Earthworms move in. They turn the soil over just as a shovel does.

They burrow down and break up the soil just as a rake does.

In about ten years the rotting log has become a mound of rich, black earth.

One autumn day an acorn falls
from a nearby oak tree.
A squirrel buries it in the rich soil.

A seedling oak sprouts . . .
and grows . . .
and grows until . . .

one day deep in the forest
another great oak tree stands.

Squirrels move in.
So do carpenter ants, beetles, and woodpeckers.

The ants build nests.
The beetles burrow.
The woodpeckers peck.
For years life goes on in the oak tree.

Then one night
the wind whistles through the trees.
The old oak bends and shakes.
It crashes to the forest floor.

And becomes
another giant log.